The Cat Lover's Cookbook

D1572719

The Cat Lover's Cookbook

Eighty-five
Fast, Economical, and Healthy
Recipes for Your Cat

Franki B. Papai

Illustrations by Art Decker

St. Martin's Press
New York

For Roxy

I'd like to dedicate this book to my cat
Who fell from the sky, right into my lap.
For without my cat this book would not be
I love you, Roxy Weasel Cooch Magee. (a.k.a *The Hairy One.*)

The Cat Lover's Cookbook. Copyright © 1993 by Franki B. Papai. All rights reserved. Printed in the United States of America. No part of this book may be used or reproduced in any manner whatsoever without written permission except in the case of brief quotations embodied in critical articles or reviews. For information, address St. Martin's Press, 175 Fifth Avenue, New York, N.Y. 10010

Illustrations by Art Decker

ISBN 0-312-08904-X

First U.S. Edition: April 1993

10 9 8 7 6 5 4 3 2 1

Categories

Acknowledgments

A special thanks to all those who helped make this book possible:

Tony Secunda, for unlimited inspiration and true dedication;

Dr. Thomas Schwarzmann, for his love of cats and his professional advice;

Art Decker, for his art, of course, and for his good advice throughout the project;

Barbara Anderson, my editor at St. Martin's Press;

Carolyn Miller, for editorial services;

Beverly Dubin, for her portrait photo;

Andrew Leranth, **Futzie Nutzle** and **Halina**, **Billy** and **Marcy Somogyi**, **Terrie** and **George Pagan**, and, of course, my cat **Roxy**.

Thank You.

—Franki B. Papai

Foreword

It is fair to assume that our cats would enjoy a tasty, home-cooked meal as much as we do. However, we cannot assume that cats have the same dietary and nutritional needs as humans. Their needs *are* different, but with the help of Franki Papai's *The Cat Lover's Cookbook*, you will learn how to create tasty meals that provide a complete and balanced diet for your cat, no matter what his or her age.

If you make sure to use a variety of recipes from this feline cookbook, you can replace commercial canned cat foods. The book's recipes can also be used to supplement and add variety to your cat's canned foods. But no matter which approach you take, you'll find that it's more nutritious and much more economical to provide home-prepared foods for your cat. And your cat will appreciate your efforts!

Before introducing home-cooked meals into your cat's diet, you should become familiar with the nutritional information and the preparation guidelines outlined on pages 3–7. You might also want to check with your veterinarian, especially if your cat is pregnant, old, or suffering from any type of medical problem. Be sure to observe your cat's appearance and behavior as you introduce this new diet. You should become concerned if there is any interruption of the regular and predictable behavior pattern. Any nutritional concern or question, and any digestive-tract disturbance (for example, vomiting, diarrhea, or skipping one or two meals) should be addressed by the most qualified resource—your veterinarian.

Now, buoyed with the anticipation that your cat can benefit from home-cooked meals, isn't it time to share some taste treats with your feline friend? *Bon apetit!*

—Thomas Schwarzmann, D.V.M.

Introduction

We all know that cat lovers will stop at nothing to make sure that the feline members of their family are as healthy and well taken care of as possible. It is for this kind of concerned and attentive reader that I present the recipes in this book. Each one has been carefully researched and reviewed by a licensed veterinarian to ensure that it will meet all of your feline's nutritional needs. My goal has been to make each recipe nutritionally sound, yet easy to prepare and much more economical than canned cat food. In fact, these recipes are so nutritious and so free of preservatives and other questionable substances found in most commercial foods, that you couldn't find their equivalent in a can—at any price!

With a little practice and just a little extra effort, you'll find that homemade is by far the healthiest way to feed your cat. So why wait? Try one of these recipes for your cat's next meal and experience the results for yourself!

Your Cat's Special Nutritional Needs

There is tremendous variation among cats in terms of size, personality, and activity level, but fortunately there are some general guidelines that can be applied to feline nutrition.

The average (ten-pound, unstressed, active) cat requires 350–400 calories per day to maintain his or her weight. This is approximately the number of calories contained in 4 ounces of dry cat food or two 6-ounce cans of cat food. It may not seem like much when compared to the 1500–2500 calories consumed by adult cat owners, but be assured that it is adequate for a cat, provided those 350 calories supply the right nutrients.

The amount a cat eats changes during the various stages of his or her life. It also varies from cat to cat, depending on the amount of exercise and energy expended. If your cat is experiencing stress due to illness, postoperative surgery, pregnancy, lactation, or cold weather, his or her calorie requirement can increase by 50–100 percent (roughly 500–700 calories per day). Your goal should be to maintain your cat's ideal weight; periodically weigh your cat* and watch for changes in his or her curves and silhouette. The amount of food should be carefully and gradually increased or decreased accordingly. If you notice dramatic or rapid weight changes, a checkup by your veterinarian is in order. The following charts show the special calorie requirements for various stages of your cat's life, and the calorie content of various foods.

Feline Calorie Requirements for Each Stage of Life	
Stage of Life	Daily Calorie Requirement for Each Pound of Body Weight
Kitten (4–10 weeks)	113
Kitten (5 months)	59
Kitten (7 months)	45
Kitten (9 months)	36
Inactive adult cat	32
Active adult cat	36
Pregnant cat	45
Lactating cat	56–145

*The easiest way to weigh your cat is to weigh yourself first, pick up your cat, and reweigh yourself holding your cat.

3

Calorie Content of Various Foods

Protein	Calories per ½ Cup	Protein	Calories per ½ Cup
Beef, raw (lean chuck)	199	Salmon, baked (no bones)	149
Beef liver, raw	137	Salmon, canned (drained)	130
Beef heart, raw	148	Salmon, smoked (¼ cup)	180
Beef kidney, raw	122	Shrimp, cooked (¼ cup)	65
Beef, broiled (lean ground)	217	Crab, cooked (shelled)	86
Beef, fried (lean ground)	234	Clams, canned (¼ cup, drained)	40
Beef bouillon cube	8	Kippered fillet, canned	
Lamb, raw (lean from leg)	117	(2 tablespoons, drained)	175
Lamb, raw (lean ground)	275	Sardine, canned in oil	172
Chicken, baked with skin	150	Flounder, cooked (4 ounces,	
Chicken, baked with no skin	128	no bones)	130
Chicken neck, simmered (meat only)	32	Sole, baked (no bones)	100
Chicken liver (one whole liver)	41	Other basic white fish	110
Chicken wing, stewed (meat only, no skin)	43	Cottage cheese, regular (1 tablespoon)	54
Chicken wing, stewed (meat only, with skin)	100	Cottage cheese, low-fat (1 tablespoon)	13
Chicken, raw (lean ground)	150	Egg yolk, cooked	63
Chicken bouillon cube	13	Sour cream	31
Turkey, raw (lean ground)	157		

4

Calorie Content of Various Foods

Carbohydrate	Calories per ½ Cup
Brown rice, cooked	116
Barley, pearl, cooked	98
Oatmeal, cooked	72
Millet, cooked	98
Corn, cooked	89
Carrots, cooked	33
Peas, cooked	38
Bean sprouts, raw	5
Potato, cooked (medium size)	100–200
Whole wheat bread crumbs (¼ cup)	25
Dry catfood (⅓ cup or one handful)	100

Fat	Calories per Tablespoon
Beef fat	116
Chicken fat	115
Butter	102
Margarine, regular	101
Margarine, diet	56
Vegetable oils	121

In terms of the *content* of your cat's diet, the most important goal is to serve a variety of foods in the following proportion:

30 percent protein
30 percent carbohydrate
40 percent fat

Do not allow your cat to decide which foods are best; rather, work with your cat's likes and dislikes to fashion a variety of proteins, grains, vegetables, and supplements (see chart on pages 4–5) into numerous meals, which can be rotated each mealtime.

It is not absolutely necessary to give your cat a daily vitamin-mineral supplement, but it can provide valuable backup in case the nutrients in the foods you serve are not always in the right quantity or proportion for your cat. This is something to discuss with your veterinarian. If you do decide to use a vitamin-mineral supplement, include it with each of two meals per day. The chart on page 7 shows other supplements that you should consider giving to your cat; again, these should be discussed with your veterinarian.

Vitamin-Mineral Supplements

Supplement	How Often to Give and How Often to Serve It	What It Does	Where to Obtain It
Brewer's Yeast ¼ to ½ teaspoon	2 to 4 times per week, mixed into food	Good for the nervous system and high in B vitamins; also helps protect against fleas.	Health-food store
Bone Meal ¼ to ½ teaspoon	2 to 3 times per week, mixed into food	Provides calcium and minerals, both essential for your cat's health.	Drug store or health-food store
Oils ¼ to ½ teaspoon cold-pressed vegetable oil (safflower, olive, corn)	Every other day, mixed with food	Helps to provide a shiny coat and alleviate fur balls	Health-food store or supermarket
Vitamin E ¼ teaspoon vitamin E oil	2 to 3 times per week, mixed with food	Helps provide a shiny coat; also good for the immune system	Health-food store
Vitamins Vitamin-mineral supplements	Daily, mixed with meals (especially important if you serve a homemade diet)	Helps protect against potential vitamin/mineral deficiency	Veterinary clinic
Seasonings Garlic salt Onion salt Sea salt	Only to taste (pinch)	To increase palatability of regular foods	Supermarket

Adult cats require only about 350 to 400 calories per day to maintain healthy weight. Feeding your cat twice a day helps to keep him or her from becoming a finicky eater and helps prevent obesity as well as skin and digestive disorders. Each meal should average 175 to 200 calories. The calorie counts for the recipes in this book range from 25 to 800 calories. So, by providing two meals per day, and by using a wide variety of the recipes, you can be assured that you're providing adequate nutrition and calories for your cat. If a recipe contains 500 or more calories and your cat doesn't need that many calories, you can simply place half a portion in a bowl (no longer than 2 hours at room temperature) and store the other half in a covered container in the refrigerator for later that day. If your cat prefers to nibble on and off all day long, leave your homemade food out for a few hours, and then replace it with some commercial dry cat food for the rest of the day. Always be sure to provide fresh water twice a day.

Your local butcher or supermarket meat department is the best source of ingredients when cooking for your cat. In fact, the counterpeople at these places can be very helpful. If you tell them that the meats and scraps you request are for your cat, you may be pleasantly surprised with what they may provide.

What should you ask for? Here's a list of items that are available for sale (and sometimes just for the asking) at any good meat counter:

- beef and lamb hearts
- beef and lamb kidneys
- calf, beef, lamb, and chicken livers
- chicken parts, gizzards, hearts, and kidneys
- scraps or cutaways from choice sections of beef, lamb, game, chicken, or fish
- ground beef, lamb, chicken, or turkey

When you buy meats from the butcher, be sure to purchase enough for several weeks' worth of meals (this would be 2 to 3 pounds for an active adult cat). I've found that this is a great time-saver, and a money-saver as well. Chop the meats into bite-sized pieces, divide the pieces into ⅓- to ½-cup portions, put them (raw or cooked) into small freezer bags, and freeze them. By doing this, you'll be able to put together a week or even several weeks' worth of meals in just a matter of minutes. When you want to cook for your cat, take a bag out of the freezer the night before and place in the refrigerator so that it will thaw, or put one into the microwave to defrost. If you decide to cook the meat before you freeze it, then I suggest you sauté the meat in a small skillet with 1 tablespoon of cold-pressed vegetable oil (add a pinch of salt for taste) and cook for 2 minutes. Drain off the oil, and cool the meat before placing it in the freezer bag.

You'll just love how easy it is to cook these recipes, and your cat will love the quality of the food, and no doubt will repay you in kind with much affection. Best of all, it's cheaper to cook for your cat than it is to buy canned cat food. So try one of these recipes on your cat today and see the results for yourself. It may take a little extra time, but your reward will be a healthy, happy cat.

Here are some additional tips and techniques for keeping your cat—and you—happy at mealtimes:

1. Find one place where your cat can eat all his or her meals. It should be protected from intrusions by small toddlers, strangers, or other animals.

2. Make sure the food you feed your cat is fresh.

3. Use easily cleaned durable plastic or ceramic dishes. If there is more than one cat in the house, see that each cat has his or her own bowl so you can keep an eye on each one's eating habits.

4. Make sure your cat's bowl or dish is clean before you add more food. Don't leave any soggy residues.

5. Always introduce new foods gradually. Mix small amounts into well-liked foods and slowly increase the amount of the new food over several weeks.

6. For the sake of your cat's digestion, serve food lukewarm or at room temperature. Cats don't like food either too hot or too cold.

7. Provide fresh water for your cat at least twice a day, both indoors and outdoors, and especially in the winter when inside air can be very dry. This will discourage the cat from drinking from unhealthy sources.

8. We all know that our cat is "purrfect," though sometimes his or her table

manners are not. Try putting a newspaper under your cat's dishes. This will keep the floor clean and will make spills easy to clean. Once a week, just fold up the paper, throw it away, and replace it with new paper. I find the Sunday comic section looks great. A sheet of paper towel also makes a great placemat.

9. Raw egg *yolk* two times a week mixed into food is o.k.; however, raw egg *white* contains avitin, which destroys biotin, a vitamin B complex that is essential to a cat's health and well-being. **Never** give raw egg whites *in any form* to your cat.

10. For a special treat, get some catnip from your local pet shop or health-food store. It's also easy to grow a plant of catnip in the garden. There are several ways to use catnip:

   ● Tie some up in a small cloth to make a toy.

   ● Use it to make tea: Steep 1 teaspoon catnip in 1 cup hot water for 3 minutes. Let cool before serving (to your cat!).

   ● Your cat will love catnip, and you are sure to be loved in return.

11. If you've just had the pleasure of getting a new kitten, take special care in developing his or her character.

   ● Feeding your kitten a midnight snack is a great idea if you do not want to be awakened very early the next day. Or leave a small bowl of high-quality dry cat food, so your kitten can nibble on and off throughout the night.

   ● Try taking a walk with your kitten, using a leash and collar.

   ● Make sure to visit your veterinarian with your kitten at 8 weeks of age. Vaccination shots and worming at 2 months are very important. Follow your veterinarian's recommendations for follow-up visits.

   ● Provide plenty of healthy meals and lots of love and attention.

12. If you have just found a cat, look for lost-cat notices. To prevent losing your own cat, have a good snapshot of your cat ready—just in case, so you can use it on a poster to identify him or her. You should provide the date you lost your cat, a contact number, and a clear, well-written description of your cat. An identification tag attached to his or her collar, which should include his/her name, your name, address, and phone number is also a good idea— even for indoor cats.

13. For overall cat health:

    • Carefully watch the degree of luster and the amount of shedding of your cat's coat. Except for seasonal shedding and thickening, any change, even gradual, can be a sign of trouble. A two-minute brushing once a day will give your cat immense pleasure and will help keep the fleas away, prevent hair balls, and will give a nice appearance to your cat's coat.

    • Please make sure that your cat visits the veterinarian for checkups and yearly shots. This is a most-important step to ensure that your kitty has a long and healthy life.

Breakfast

For some cats this meal is a favorite; for others, the first meal of the day is of only mild interest. Cat owners can easily notice the pattern of their cat's activity and appetite, and can plan the calorie content and size of the meals accordingly. All meals in this book are perishable and should not be left out for more than 2 hours at room temperature. If your feline likes frequent snacks, the solution is to leave out a handful of a high-quality dry cat food. Although each cat differs in terms of how much activity he or she likes and how much sleep he or she needs, most cats will adapt quite easily to two meals per day, presented in the morning and evening. The key to a successful feeding regimen (for a happy cat) is a balanced, varied diet, fresh water daily, and food dishes that are washed after every meal. You should also wash the water bowl with dish detergent at least every few days. In other words, your cat will benefit most from a variety of meals cooked from the recipes in this book.

Hair of the Cat

1 egg, boiled 6 minutes
3 tablespoons smoked salmon, minced
1 teaspoon low-fat sour cream

Cut the egg into bite-sized pieces. Mix the egg, salmon, and sour cream together in a bowl. Serve.

Yield: 2 meals; 190 calories per meal.

Finally Flounder

4 ounces flounder fillet
½ teaspoon olive oil
1 egg, boiled 6 minutes
1 teaspoon grated Parmesan cheese

Brush the fish with the olive oil. Broil for about 2 minutes per side. The fish should flake with a fork when done. Cut the egg into bite-sized pieces. Mash the fish with a fork and mix with the egg in a bowl. Top with grated cheese. Serve warm, not hot.

Yield: 2 meals; 165 calories per meal.

A Dandy Omelette

2 eggs
1 tablespoon milk
1 tablespoon safflower oil
1 tablespoon mushrooms, minced
¼ cup cooked spinach, minced
1 tablespoon Cheddar cheese, grated

In a bowl, beat the eggs with the milk. Place the oil in a small skillet and heat over medium heat. Add the egg mixture and cook for 2 minutes. With a spatula, lift the edges and underside of the egg so that it can be folded over. Sprinkle the mushrooms on top of the eggs. Add the spinach and sprinkle with grated cheese. Fold the omelette in half, remove it from the skillet, and let cool. Cut into bite-sized pieces. Serve in a bowl, warm, not hot.

Yield: 2 meals; 200 calories per meal.

Crunchy Surprise

  1 handful high-quality dry cat food
  2 tablespoons cooked beef, minced
  1 egg yolk
  1 teaspoon warm milk

Place the dry cat food in a bowl and mix in the minced beef. Stir in the egg yolk and pour the warm milk over the mixture. Serve.

Yield: 2 meals; 225 calories per meal.

Kitty Bran

  1 handful high-quality dry cat food
  1 tablespoon Miller's bran (from health-food
    store)
  1 tablespoon warm milk

Place the dry cat food in a bowl. Add the Miller's bran. Pour the warm milk on top of the bran and stir. Serve.

Yield: 1 meal; 145 calories.

Champion Breakfast

  1 to 2 tablespoons safflower oil
  4 ounces ground beef, chicken, or turkey
  dash garlic salt
  2 eggs
  1 tablespoon steamed carrots, minced
  1 teaspoon cottage cheese

Heat the oil in a small skillet over medium heat. Cook the meat for 2 minutes and add the garlic salt. In a bowl, mix the eggs, vegetable, and cottage cheese. Add to the pan. Cook for 3 minutes, stirring often. Place in a bowl and serve warm, not hot.

Yield: 2 meals; 260 calories per meal for chicken and turkey, 325 calories per meal for beef.

No Fui Tofui

⅓ cup cooked brown rice
½ cup cooked corn
2 ounces tofu (raw or lightly sauteed in butter or tamari)
1 egg yolk

In a bowl, mix the brown rice and corn. Cut the tofu into bite-sized pieces and mix into the rice mixture along with the egg yolk. Serve.

Yield: 2 meals; 300 calories per meal.

Kipper Delight

3 soda crackers
3 tablespoons kippered herring
1 teaspoon sour cream

Break up the soda crackers in a bowl. Mash the herring with a fork and add to the crackers. Mix in the sour cream and serve.

Yield: 1 meal; 210 calories.

Shrimp Cottage

1 egg, boiled 6 minutes
⅓ cup cooked shrimp, minced
2 teaspoons cottage cheese

Cut the egg into bite-sized pieces, place in a bowl, and add the shrimp and cottage cheese. Mix and serve.

Yield: 1 meal; 240 calories.

Tutti Fruitti

1 teaspoon cantaloupe, minced
1 teaspoon watermelon, minced
1 teaspoon seedless grapes, minced
2 teaspoons cottage cheese

In a bowl, combine the fruit and cottage cheese. Serve as a treat.

Yield: 1 treat; 10 calories.

19

The most critical nutrient for all living beings is water. Most cats will voluntarily consume the amount of water their bodies need. It is an absolute necessity to provide fresh water in a clean bowl—daily. Cats living in either very hot or especially cold climates will benefit from a diet supplemented with occasional soup meals. Cats seem to drink less water when the weather is cold even though physiological needs are constant. To avoid dehydration, especially for older cats, male cats, and cats with kidney disease, a soup meal will provide a little extra fluid intake. Remember, it is more appropriate to a cat's health and metabolism to use water instead of milk when providing liquids to cats. Small amounts of milk (1 teaspoon daily) are tolerated by a cat's digestive systems, but it is wiser to provide milk on an infrequent basis. Milk in greater amounts usually leads to diarrhea since a cat is unable to digest milk sugars. Cats recovering from an illness or surgery, cats with compromised kidney function, older cats (over 10 years of age), cats with gum disease, and cats fighting off respiratory illness benefit from soup meals. The recipes in this chapter are easy to prepare and will help ensure that your cat consumes enough liquids. You will be pleasantly surprised how much your feline enjoys them!

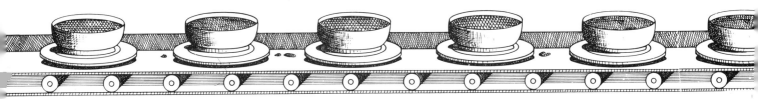

Tail-Wagger Vegetable Soup

1 cup water
1 vegetable bouillon cube (low-sodium)
½ cup cooked barley or brown rice
½ cup steamed vegetables (carrots, cauliflower, or peas), minced

Boil the water in a small saucepan, add the bouillon cube, and stir to dissolve. Lower the heat to a simmer and add the barley or rice and vegetables to soup. Mix well and cook for 2 minutes. Serve in a bowl, warm not hot.

Yield: 1 meal; 175 calories.

Purrfect Turkey Soup

1 cup water
1 chicken bouillon cube (low-sodium)
⅛ teaspoon garlic powder (optional)
½ teaspoon steamed bone meal
½ cup cooked turkey, chopped
⅓ cup steamed cabbage, chopped

Boil the water in a small sauce pan, add the bouillon cube, and stir to dissolve. Lower the heat to a simmer. Add the garlic powder and the steamed bone meal. Stir in the turkey and mix thoroughly. Cool. Add the cooked cabbage and heat for 1 minute. Serve in a bowl, warm not hot.

Yield: 1 meal; 180 calories.

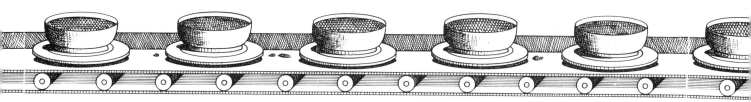

Kitty Clam-up

1½ tablespoons milk
¼ cup canned minced clams, drained
¼ cup clam juice (from can)
2 tablespoons cooked potato, peeled and minced
1 drop lemon juice

In a small saucepan, combine all of the ingredients and heat. Serve in a bowl, warm not hot.

Yield: 1 meal; 125 calories.

Fish Stew

⅓ cup low-sodium V8 juice
¼ cup canned minced clams, drained
1 cup water
¼ cup clam juice (from can)
1 tablespoon bell pepper, minced
¼ cup shrimp, minced
¼ cup boned white fish, minced

In a medium saucepan stir together V8 juice, clams, water, and clam juice. Add the bell pepper and cook for 2 minutes over medium heat. Add the shrimp and fish. Cook for 5 minutes. Serve in a bowl, warm not hot.

Yield: 1 meal; 200 calories.

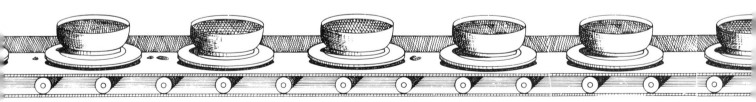

Siamese Surprise

1 cup water
1 vegetable, beef, or chicken bouillon cube
  (low-sodium)
1 egg, beaten
1 tablespoon steamed peas
1 clove garlic, crushed
1 sliver fresh ginger, minced
1 water chestnut, minced
½ teaspoon steamed bone meal

Boil the water in a small saucepan, add the bouillon cube, and stir to dissolve. Lower the heat to a simmer and add the egg, peas, garlic, ginger, and water chestnut. Stir in the steamed bone meal. Simmer for 2 minutes. Serve in a bowl, warm not hot.

Yield: 1 meal; 120 calories.

Hearty Stew

⅔ cup water
½ cup gravy (homemade)
½ cup mixed vegetables, steamed
½ cup cooked beef or chicken, minced
2 tablespoons cooked potato, peeled and
  chopped

Mix all of the ingredients in a saucepan and cook over low heat until warm. Serve in a bowl, warm not hot.

Yield: 2 meals; 150 calories per meal for chicken, 210 calories per meal for beef.

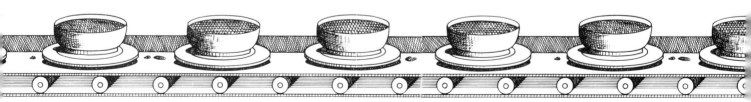

Soothing Cool Soup

1   cup water
1   tablespoon ground dried alfalfa leaves (from health-food store)
1   tablespoon dried peppermint leaves
1   sliver fresh ginger
¼   teaspoon honey

Boil the water in a saucepan and turn off the heat. Add the alfalfa, mint, and ginger. Steep for 5 minutes. Add the honey and stir. Strain through a tea sieve into a bowl. Cool. Serve as a treat.

Yield: 1 treat; 25 calories.

Something Fishy

½   cup boned white fish, cooked
⅔   cup chicken broth
¼   teaspoon garlic, minced

In a saucepan, mash the fish with a fork, then stir in broth and garlic. Simmer for 2 minutes. Add water if needed. Serve in a bowl, warm not hot.

Yield: 1 meal; 110 calories.

Chicken or Veggie Noodle Soup

1   cup water
1   chicken or vegetable bouillon cube (low-sodium)
½   cup cooked chicken, chopped
½   cup cooked whole wheat spaghetti, minced
¼   cup steamed carrots, peas, corn, or green beans, minced

In a small saucepan, boil the water, add the bouillon cube, and stir to dissolve. Lower the heat, add the chicken, spaghetti, and vegetables. Cook until tender. Serve in a bowl, warm not hot.

Yield: 1 meal; 225 calories.

Fish

The most important principle to follow when feeding fish to your cat is to cook the fish before serving it. Raw fish contains thiaminase, an enzyme that destroys thiamin (vitamin B-1), which can lead to a deficiency of this vitamin that often results in neurological disease. Also, raw fish contains parasites that are harmful to cats; the cooking process kills potential parasites.

You may notice that your cat develops a particular taste for fish; however, it is important to provide protein from a variety of animal sources (beef, poultry, dairy) in your cat's diet. So use these recipes in moderation and remember that variety is the spice of life!

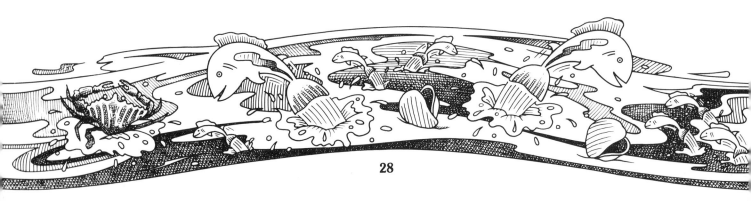

Shipmate Surprise

2 cups fish broth, chicken broth, or water
1 fish head with 1-inch meat attached
½ cup celery, chopped
¼ cup carrot, chopped
¾ cup cooked brown rice
½ teaspoon cod liver oil

In a saucepan, bring the broth or water to a boil. Add the fish head. Cook for 1 minute. Add the celery and carrot. Cook for 20 minutes, or until the vegetables are tender. With a large slotted spoon, lift the fish head out of the liquid. Transfer to a plate and let cool completely. Transfer the vegetables into a serving bowl and let cool. Reserve the cooking liquid. Add the cooked rice to the vegetables and mix. Add the cod liver oil and stir. When fish head is completely cooled, pull the meat from the bone and mash the fish meat with a fork. Make sure the fish has no bones, then add it to the bowl of vegetables and rice. Add just enough reserved liquid to make a little gravy. Serve warm, not hot.

Yield: 2 meals; 175 calories per meal.

Kitty Captain's Plate

⅔ cup boned fish, cooked
1 tablespoon cooked peas
1 tablespoon cooked carrots, minced
2 teaspoons cottage cheese
½ teaspoon steamed bone meal (optional)

In a bowl, mash the fish with a fork. Add the vegetables to the fish and mix well. Add the cottage cheese and lightly mix together. If adding the steamed bone meal, mix in. Serve.

Yield: 1 meal; 265 calories.

All-night Stir Fry

½ teaspoon cod liver oil or safflower oil
1 tablespoon broccoli, minced
1 tablespoon carrots, minced
¼ teaspoon soy sauce (low-sodium)
1 sliver fresh ginger, minced
3 tablespoons cooked shrimp, chopped

Heat the oil in a wok or skillet over high heat. Add the broccoli and carrots, and cook until tender. Mix in the soy sauce and ginger. Add the shrimp and cook for 1 minute. Serve warm, not hot.

Yield: 1 meal; 165 calories.

Ocean Delight

3 tablespoons dried bread crumbs
1 egg yolk
1 small haddock fillet (about 4 ounces)
1 teaspoon safflower oil

Preheat the oven to 350°F. Spread the bread crumbs on a plate. Beat the egg yolk in a bowl and dip the fish into the egg. Lift the fish out of the egg yolk and coat the fish with the bread crumbs. Add the oil to a small baking pan. Place the fish in the pan and bake for 15 minutes on each side. Remove fish to a dish, let cool, and cut into bite-sized pieces. You may want to add a little mayonnaise to moisten.

Yield: 1 meal; 200 calories.

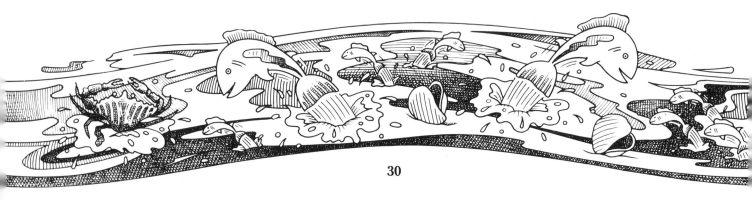

Sir Sardiney

4 canned sardines, drained
½ teaspoon oil from sardine can
⅓ cup cooked brown rice
2 teaspoons cottage cheese

In a bowl, mash the fish and oil with a fork. Add the brown rice and cottage cheese. Stir together. Serve.

Yield: 1 meal; 130 calories.

Aye-aye Kipper

2 eggs
1 tablespoon bell pepper, minced
2 canned kipper fillets, drained
1 teaspoon safflower oil

Beat the eggs in a bowl and add the bell pepper. Mash the fish with a fork or cut into bite-sized pieces and stir into the egg mixture. Heat the oil in a small skillet over low heat. Add the egg mixture. Cook and stir until the egg is scrambled. Serve warm, not hot.

Yield: 2 meals; 210 calories per meal.

Crab Delight

½ cup cooked crab meat, shredded
½ cup steamed vegetables (broccoli, spinach, or carrots), minced
1 teaspoon brewer's yeast
½ teaspoon safflower oil
3 eggs, beaten
1 teaspoon milk
⅓ cup Cheddar cheese, grated

In a bowl, mix the crab meat, vegetables, and brewer's yeast. Spread the oil over the bottom of a pie plate and add the crab and vegetable mixture. In a bowl, combine the eggs, milk, and cheese. Pour over the crab mixture. Bake in a preheated 350°F oven until firm, about 30 minutes. Cut into bite-sized pieces. Serve warm, not hot.

Yield: 2 meals; 390 calories per meal.

Yammie Fish

1 small cooked yam, peeled
½ cup cooked fish, boned
2 handfuls high-quality dry cat food
1 teaspoon warm milk

In a bowl, mash together the yam and fish. Add the dry cat food and pour the warm milk over mixture and stir. Serve.

Yield: 2 meals; 175 calories per meal.

Mr. Soleful

1 teaspoon safflower oil
4 ounces sole fillet
⅔ cup fish broth or vegetable broth
¼ teaspoon flour
½ teaspoon heavy (whipping) cream
2 drops lemon juice
¼ teaspoon fresh parsley, minced

Preheat the oven to 350°F. Place the oil in a small baking pan, add the sole, and bake for 3 minutes per side. Remove the pan from the oven and set aside. In a small saucepan, stir together the broth, flour, and cream. Place the saucepan over low heat and cook until the mixture thickens slightly. Place the fish on a serving plate and cut into bite-sized pieces. Pour the sauce over the fish. Add a couple drops of lemon juice and sprinkle the parsley on top. Serve warm, not hot.

Yield: 1 meal; 200 calories.

Entrees

Entree usually applies to the main feature of a meal. In this cookbook, however, every recipe represents a nutritious meal for your cat. The concept of a complete diet depends on feeding your cat a variety of recipes over the course of the week. In other words, the recipes in this chapter can (but need not) be considered week-to-week mainstays for your cat's home-cooked diet. The recipes provide sound nutrition for a cat at any stage of life; you can adjust the serving size slightly if your cat has special needs (more food if she is pregnant or lactating, for example; less food if he or she is overweight). Either way you can be sure of a healthy entree for your cat. *Bon apetit!*

Go, Cats, Go

   1 teaspoon safflower oil
   1 lamb kidney
   ¼ teaspoon garlic, crushed
   ½ teaspoon steamed bone meal
   1 tablespoon cottage cheese

Heat the oil in a skillet. Chop the kidney into bite-sized pieces. Add the garlic and kidney to the skillet and sauté the mixture for 2 minutes. Stir in the steamed bone meal. Transfer to a bowl and let cool. Stir in the cottage cheese. Serve warm, not hot.

Yield: 1 meal; 175 calories.

Tabby Magnifico

   1 egg, boiled 5 minutes
   3 tablespoons boned salmon, cooked
   2 teaspoons cottage cheese
   1 to 2 tablespoons wheat germ

Place the egg and the salmon in a bowl and mash them together with a fork. Stir in the cottage cheese and wheat germ. Serve.

Yield: 2 meals; 230 calories per meal.

Cat's Pajamas

   ⅓ cup cooked beef, minced
   ¼ to ⅓ cup cooked brown rice or barley
   2 tablespoons steamed vegetables, minced
   1 tablespoon leftover gravy (or add 1 tablespoon
      water to 1 tablespoon instant gravy)

Stir all the ingredients together. Serve.

Yield: 2 meals; 270 calories per serving.

Kitty Canton

⅓ cup tofu
½ teaspoon peanut oil
1 clove garlic, minced
½ teaspoon soy sauce (low-sodium)
2 tablespoons steamed vegetables, minced
1 vegetable bouillon cube (low-sodium), dissolved in ¼ cup hot water
1 teaspoon fresh alfalfa sprouts

Chop the tofu into bite-sized pieces. Heat the oil in a skillet over medium heat. Brown the tofu and garlic for about 2 minutes. Stir in the soy sauce and add the vegetables. Lower the heat to a simmer and cook for 2 minutes. Stir in the broth. Remove the pan from the heat and let cool for 1 minute. Chop the alfalfa sprouts in little pieces. Add to the pan and stir. Serve.

Yield: 1 meal; 280 calories.

Liver Lover

½ teaspoon olive oil
4 ounces calf's liver
1 teaspoon canned tomatoes, drained (or 1 teaspoon fresh tomato, chopped and peeled)
⅓ cup cooked barley
Pinch salt

Heat the oil in a skillet over medium heat. Chop the liver into bite-sized pieces and add to pan. Lower heat to simmer and cook the liver for 1 minute. Mash the tomato and add to the pan. Stir in the barley and add a pinch of salt. Serve warm, not hot.

Yield: 1 meal; 220 calories.

Pounce-burger with Cheese

½ cup ground beef, chicken, or lamb
1 tablespoon undiluted cream of mushroom soup
1 egg yolk
⅓ cup bread crumbs
1 thin slice (2 ounces) organic cheese (from health-food store)

In a bowl, combine the meat, soup, egg yolk, and bread crumbs. Form into a patty and broil for 3 minutes on each side. Place the cheese slice on top and broil until the cheese melts. Place in a serving bowl, mash up a bit, and serve warm, not hot.

Yield: 2 meals; 240 calories per meal.

Have a Heart

1 teaspoon safflower oil
½ teaspoon bell pepper, minced
3 tablespoons beef heart, minced
1 tablespoon cottage cheese

Heat the oil in a skillet over medium heat. Add the bell pepper and sauté until tender. Stir the beef heart into the skillet and brown for 2 minutes. Transfer to a serving bowl and let cool. Stir in the cottage cheese. Serve.

Yield: 1 meal; 200 calories.

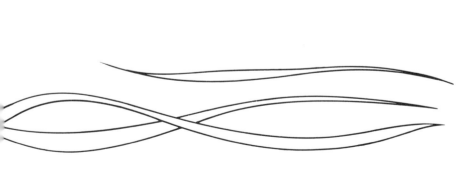

Pawsta with Sauce

½ teaspoon safflower oil
¼ teaspoon garlic, crushed
¼ cup mushrooms, minced
4 ounces ground beef or poultry
1 teaspoon tomato sauce
⅓ cup cooked whole wheat spaghetti, chopped

Heat the oil in a skillet over medium heat. Add the garlic and mushrooms. Sauté until tender. Add the ground meat and mix well. Simmer for 2 minutes. Add the tomato sauce and mix well. Stir in the spaghetti. Place in a serving bowl. Serve warm, not hot.

Yield: 2 meals; 150 calories per meal for chicken, 210 calories per meal for beef.

Bengal Cat

7 tablespoons chicken broth
⅓ cup cooked brown rice, or ½ cup cooked oatmeal
1 teaspoon safflower oil
½ teaspoon steamed bone meal
½ cup cooked lamb (fat trimmed), minced
¼ cup cooked spinach, chopped

Heat the broth in a saucepan over low heat. Stir in the rice or oatmeal, oil, and steamed bone meal. Cook until warm. Stir in the lamb and spinach. Cook for 2 minutes. Serve warm, not hot.

Yield: 2 meals; 360 calories per meal for brown rice, 400 calories per meal for oatmeal.

Roving Romeo

Tomcats are unaltered male cats of any age. Testosterone, a male hormone that circulates in their blood stream tends to dominate much of their activity. Tomcats are especially aggressive toward other male cats (altered or unaltered). Tomcats tend to wander, and often stay away from home for days. They are inclined to fight with other cats, and generally expend more calories than either neutered males or females. Often tomcats are thin and in poor condition. Surgical castration will usually alleviate the cat's tendency to roam and fight, and he will become much more affectionate. If castration is not an option, a more energy-dense diet and/or a greater quantity of food may keep the cat in better condition. When your tomcat finally comes home—and before he goes out again, he will need plenty of food. Here are some recipes that are high in calories and great in nutritional value for your roving romeo.

On the Prowl

½ teaspoon safflower oil
1 tablespoon bell pepper, minced
3 tablespoons cooked potato, peeled and diced
½ cup ground beef

Heat the oil in a small skillet over medium heat. Sauté the bell pepper until tender. Add the potato and mix in. Add the ground beef and cook, stirring constantly for about 5 minutes. Serve warm, not hot.

Yield: 2 meals; 200 calories per meal.

Alley Cat Surprise

½ cup water
1 whole chicken liver, chopped
1 tablespoon beef kidney, chopped
1 teaspoon cottage cheese

In a saucepan, boil the water and add the liver and kidney. Cook for 2 minutes. In a bowl, combine the cooked liver and kidney, and the cottage cheese. Serve warm, not hot.

Yield: 1 meal; 175 calories.

Envy of the Block

3 tablespoons boned salmon, cooked
1 hard-boiled egg, chopped
1 teaspoon mayonnaise
½ teaspoon brewer's yeast

In a bowl, mash the fish with a fork. Stir in the egg. In a separate bowl, stir together the mayonnaise and brewer's yeast, then stir into fish mixture. Serve.

Yield: 2 meals; 235 calories per meal.

Top Cats

4 ounces cooked beef heart, chopped into
   bite-sized pieces
1 tablespoon cooked green beans, minced
½ teaspoon olive oil
⅓ cup cooked brown rice
½ teaspoon soy sauce (low-sodium)

In a saucepan, combine all the ingredients. Warm the mixture through. Serve warm, not hot.

Yield: 2 meals; 225 calories per meal.

Hair Raiser

1 tablespoon spaghetti sauce (not too spicy)
½ cup cooked whole wheat spaghetti, chopped
1 slice leftover garlic bread
2 teaspoons grated Italian cheese

Warm the sauce and spaghetti in a saucepan. Place the slice of garlic bread in a bowl, pour the sauce over the bread, and let it sit for 2 minutes, or until bread is soggy. Break the bread into bite-sized pieces and sprinkle with the grated cheese. Serve warm, not hot.

Yield: 1 meal; 230 calories.

Lover's Lunch

½ cup cooked shrimp (no shell), chopped
1 hard-boiled egg, chopped
⅓ cup canned corn
1 teaspoon sour cream

In a bowl, combine all the ingredients. Serve.

Yield: 1 meal; 305 calories.

Tail Wagger

⅓ cup cooked chicken, chopped
2 tablespoons mixed steamed vegetables, chopped
⅓ cup cooked millet
1 teaspoon cottage cheese

In a bowl, combine all of the ingredients. Serve as a treat.

Yield: 1 treat; 130 calories.

Hair of the Cat

1 cooked chicken liver, chopped
3 canned sardines, drained
¼ teaspoon oil from sardine can
1 egg yolk, cooked
1 teaspoon brewer's yeast

In a bowl, mash the liver and fish with oil. In a separate bowl, mash the cooked egg yolk with the brewer's yeast, then add to liver and fish. Combine and serve.

Yield: 1 meal; 225 calories.

The Purrfect Night Out

¼ cup cooked lamb, chopped
¼ cup cooked beef, chopped
1 egg yolk
⅓ cup cooked barley
1 teaspoon cottage cheese
1 tablespoon steamed vegetable, chopped
1 teaspoon brewer's yeast

In a bowl, combine the meat, egg yolk, barley, cottage cheese, and vegetable. Sprinkle the brewer's yeast on top, then mix it in. Serve.

Yield: 4 meals; 200 calories per meal.

43

Mothers To Be and Nursing Mothers

Two frequent mistakes made by cat owners of pregnant and nursing mothers are supplementing the cat's diet with calcium or dairy protein (milk, cottage cheese, yogurt) and underfeeding the lactating cat. Realize that both pregnant and lactating cats have greater calorie needs. The required food increases are 125 percent for pregnant cats and 200 percent for a lactating mother. These physiologic needs should be met by feeding your mother cat the appropriate amounts of food. Any mineral (calcium) supplements should be provided only on the advice of a veterinarian. Once the kittens are at weaning age (4 weeks) and consuming solid food, the mother cat should be gradually weaned from her previously calorie-rich diet over a period of 2–4 weeks. All these recipes are veterinarian-approved for your cat. It's a special time for your mother to be and nursing mother, so the right diet is very important. If you have any doubts, seek professional advice from your veterinarian.

Surprise, Surprise

⅓ cup cooked beef liver, chopped
2 tablespoons carrots, beets, or leafy greens, minced
1 egg yolk
1 teaspoon brewer's yeast
2 handfuls high-quality dry cat food

In a bowl, mix all the ingredients together except the dry cat food. Stir in the dry cat food and serve.

Yield: 2 meals; 225 calories per meal.

Eating for Six

⅔ cup cooked chicken, chopped
1 teaspoon mayonnaise
2 tablespoons steamed vegetables, chopped
1 teaspoon steamed bone meal

In a bowl, combine the chicken, mayonnaise, and vegetables. Stir in the bone meal. Serve.

Yield: 1 meal; 175 calories.

Feline Delight

⅓ cup cooked spinach, chopped
⅓ cup cooked grain (oatmeal, brown rice, or barley)
1 hard-boiled egg, chopped
1 teaspoon steamed bone meal
1 teaspoon cottage cheese

In a bowl, combine the spinach, grain, and egg. In a separate bowl, stir together the bone meal and cottage cheese then add to the spinach mixture. Stir everything together. Serve.

Yield: 2 meals; 265 calories per meal.

Beefed-up Carrots

½ cup cooked brown rice or barley
¼ cup carrot juice
¼ teaspoon garlic powder
1 hard-boiled egg, chopped
3 tablespoons cooked beef, minced

In a bowl, stir together the rice or barley, carrot juice, garlic powder, and egg. Stir in the beef and serve.

Yield: 2 meals; 330 calories per meal.

Chicken Stew

1 cup water
1 chicken bouillon cube (low-sodium)
1 cup cooked chicken, chopped
½ cup cooked vegetables (carrots, green beans, or corn), chopped
⅓ cup cooked barley
½ teaspoon steamed bone meal

Boil the water in a medium saucepan, add the bouillon cube, and stir to dissolve. Stir in the remaining ingredients. Serve warm, not hot.

Yield: 2 meals; 350 calories per meal.

No Kidding

4 tablespoons cooked kidney, chopped
½ teaspoon olive oil
1 teaspoon cottage cheese
⅓ cup cooked brown rice
1 teaspoon brewer's yeast

In a bowl, combine all of the ingredients. Serve.

Yield: 1 meal; 200 calories.

Mommie's Day

½ cup boned salmon, cooked
1 hard-boiled egg, chopped
½ teaspoon sweetened condensed milk

In a bowl, mash the salmon and egg with a fork. Stir in the milk. Serve.

Yield: 2 meals; 250 calories per meal.

Rice Deluxe

4 tablespoons cooked lamb, diced
⅓ cup cooked brown rice
1 tablespoon steamed mixed vegetables, chopped
1 tablespoon leftover gravy

In a bowl, combine the lamb and rice. Stir in the vegetables. Stir the gravy into the bowl. Serve.

Yield: 2 meals; 320 calories per meal.

The Flying Fryer

1½ cups water
1 whole chicken liver
1 whole chicken heart
1 chicken gizzard
1 tablespoon cottage cheese

Boil the water in a medium saucepan. Place the liver, heart, and gizzard in boiling water. Lower heat to medium and simmer for 1 minute. Remove liver and set aside. Continue simmering heart and gizzard for another 5 minutes. With slotted spoon, lift out the heart and gizzard and set aside to cool completely. When they have cooled, chop the liver, heart, and gizzard into bite-sized pieces. In a bowl, combine chopped meats and stir in the cottage cheese. Serve warm, not hot.

Yield: 1 meal; 180 calories.

Soda Cracker Supreme

3 soda crackers
1 teaspoon milk
4 canned sardines, drained
½ teaspoon sardine oil from can
2 teaspoons cottage cheese

In a bowl, break the cracker into small pieces. Sprinkle milk on crackers, add the sardines and oil, and mash with a fork. Stir in the cottage cheese. Serve.

Yield: 1 meal; 175 calories.

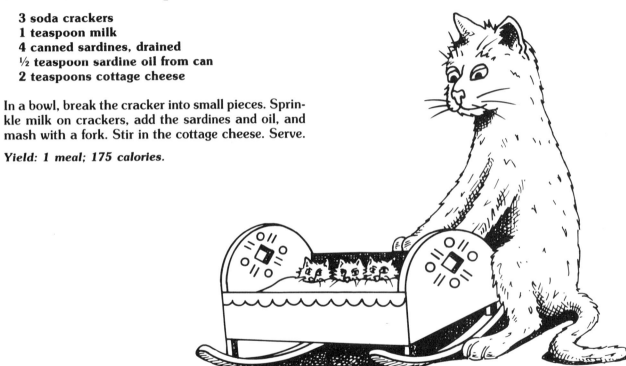

50

Kittens

A young kitten who either is not getting enough milk from his or her mother, has no mother, or is being outcompeted for milk by his or her siblings, should receive a veterinarian-recommended brand of cat milk-replacement liquid nutrition (for example, KMR). A kitten in this situation should not be fed cow's milk, goat's milk, or milk from any nonfeline species. It is important to prepare each milk-replacement feeding fresh; it should not be left out since it will develop a bacterial overgrowth.

A kitten is weaned when the dietary transition from mother's milk (or the replacement milk) to solid foods has been made. For a kitten, this process naturally occurs between 4 and 8 weeks of age. Even at 3½ weeks of age, a kitten's digestive tract and his or her food-consuming abilities are capable of accommodating solid foods. After 4 weeks of age, a kitten is no longer nutritionally dependent on milk except as an extension of the weaning process or as an occasional treat. A kitten's nutritional requirements are similar to those of an adult cat; however, a kitten's metabolic needs are far greater. Whereas a mature cat's daily calorie requirement is roughly 35 calories per pound of body weight, a 10-week-old kitten requires 113 calories per pound of body weight. This decreases to 59 calories per pound of body weight at 5 months of age, and 36 calories per body weight pound at 10 months of age. Additionally, the kitten's daily protein requirement is 8.6 grams per pound of body weight, which is fully three times the adult cat's requirement of 2.9 grams. Lastly, the minimum fat requirement is 17 percent for kittens versus 10 percent for mature cats. In other words, the adult cat requires 1.5 grams of fat per pound of body weight per day; a kitten's need is 3.2 grams of fat per pound of body weight per day.

Kittens mature into adulthood between 6 months and 1 year of age. During this maturation phase, caloric requirements decrease dramatically, and there is a shift in the recommended ratio of protein to fat to carbohydrate. The adult cat's diet should be approximately: 30 percent protein, 40 percent fat, and 30 percent carbohydrate. When described as a percentage of the weight of dietary ingredients, the ratios are: 40 percent protein, 20 percent fat, and 40 percent carbohydrate. By comparison, the kitten's (age 1 month to 10 months) diet is described as approximately: 27 percent protein, 23 percent fat, and 49 percent carbohydrate. Obviously, to ensure proper growth in a kitten or young cat, precise attention must be given to dietary requirements when preparing home-cooked meals. The following recipes fit these nutritional guidelines. The recipes can also be fed as supplemental meals together with commercial kitten food. With lots of love and a well-balanced diet, your kitten should live a long and healthy life.

Kitten Nipper No. 1

⅓ cup cooked oatmeal
¼ teaspoon warm milk
¼ teaspoon honey

Place the oatmeal in a bowl. Add the warm milk to make a smooth mixture. Pour honey on top, mix, and serve warm, not hot.

Yield: 1 treat; 243 calories.

Kitten Nipper No. 2

⅓ cup cooked oatmeal
2 teaspoons steamed carrot, minced
2 small tofu chunks, diced
¼ teaspoon warm milk
2 teaspoon wheat germ

In a bowl, combine the oatmeal and carrot. Dice the tofu into bite-sized pieces and stir into the oatmeal. Blend in the warm milk and sprinkle the wheat germ on top. Serve warm, not hot.

Yield: 1 meal; 260 calories.

Wee Paws

1 teaspoon cooked chicken, minced
1 teaspoon strained vegetable baby food
1 egg yolk, cooked

In a bowl, combine the chicken and the baby food. Stir in the egg yolk. Serve.

Yield: 1 meal; 210 calories.

Itty Bitty Kitty Surprise

4 teaspoons cooked lamb, minced
1 teaspoon cooked spinach, minced
1 egg, boiled 5 minutes

In a bowl, combine the lamb and spinach. Chop the egg and stir in. Serve.

Yield: 2 meals; 130 calories per meal.

Here Puss, Puss, Puss

4 teaspoons boned white fish, cooked and minced
2 teaspoons cooked carrots, minced
½ teaspoon cottage cheese

In a bowl, combine all of the ingredients. Serve.

Yield: 1 meal; 110 calories.

Squish Squash

2 teaspoons cooked beef, minced
1 teaspoon cooked squash, chopped
¼ cup cooked brown rice

In a bowl, combine all of the ingredients. Serve.

Yield: 2 meals; 190 calories per meal.

Raw Paw Paw

2 teaspoons cooked beef kidney, minced
2 teaspoons steamed green beans or peas, minced
2 teaspoons cooked yam or potato, peeled and mashed

In a bowl, combine all of the ingredients. Serve.

Yield: 1 meal; 120 calories.

Scram Man

1 egg, scrambled
1 teaspoon steamed or raw vegetables, minced
½ teaspoon cottage cheese

In a bowl, combine all of the ingredients. Serve.

Yield: 1 meal; 175 calories.

Pre-mouse Catcher

½ cup water
1 whole chicken liver
½ teaspoon cottage cheese

In a saucepan, boil the water. Add the liver and cook for 1 minute. Remove the liver with a slotted spoon and let cool. In a bowl, mash the liver and stir in the cottage cheese. Serve.

Yield: 1 meal; 100 calories.

Puss-n-Beets

1 tablespoon cooked calf's liver, minced
½ teaspoon beets, grated
½ teaspoon carrots, grated
½ teaspoon fresh parsley, minced
1 egg yolk, cooked
2 teaspoons wheat germ

In a bowl, combine the liver, vegetables, and egg yolk. Sprinkle the wheat germ on top. Serve.

Yield: 1 meal; 175 calories.

Mighty Kitten

¼ cup cooked barley
1 tablespoon cooked zucchini, minced
1 teaspoon grated Parmesan cheese

In a bowl, combine the barley and zucchini. Top with grated cheese. Serve.

Yield: 2 meals; 190 calories per meal.

Cats are considered overweight when they exceed their optimum weight by 15 percent. As a general rule, most mature cats should weigh between 7 to 12 pounds. Some of the medical and physical problems of obesity in the feline species are: increased difficulty of movement; respiratory problems; and gastrointestinal disturbances. One weight-reducing measure is to decrease calorie intake. For cats, a guideline to safe calorie reduction is a gradual decrease (over 3 to 6 months) in calorie intake to approximately 20 to 30 percent below his or her current maintenance level. This should result in a slow, steady weight loss. This process is achieved by reducing the amount of food fed to your cat per day by 20 to 30 percent. It is extremely important that, without exception, overweight cats not be forced to lose weight quickly. Rapid weight loss in any animal is cause for concern. In addition, you should also try to increase your overweight cat's daily activity level. The recipes in this chapter are veterinarian-approved, and will ensure that your cat is receiving the right nutrients in the right proportions. You should consult a veterinarian before placing your cat on a diet.

For the Halibut

4 ounces cooked halibut fillet
1 egg, boiled 5 minutes
¼ teaspoon alfalfa sprouts, minced
3 teaspoons wheat germ

In a bowl, mash the fish with a fork. Chop the egg into bite-sized pieces and stir in the alfalfa sprouts and wheat germ. Serve.

Yield: 2 meals; 155 calories per meal.

Ounce per Pounce

3 tablespoons cooked extra-lean ground beef (oil drained)
1 tablespoon steamed broccoli tops, chopped
1 teaspoon low-fat cottage cheese

In a bowl, combine all of the ingredients. Serve.

Yield: 1 meal; 135 calories.

Low-cal Kitty

4 teaspoons cooked fish fillet
1 tablespoon steamed cauliflower, chopped
1 tablespoon steamed broccoli, chopped
¼ cup cooked spinach, chopped
¼ cup cooked brown rice
Drop lemon juice

In a bowl, combine all of the ingredients. Squeeze a drop of lemon on top. Serve.

Yield: 2 meals; 180 calories per meal.

Fruit Cattail

1 tablespoon low-fat cottage cheese
1 tablespoon cantaloupe, chopped
1 tablespoon watermelon, chopped
1 tablespoon drained canned fruit cocktail, chopped

In a bowl, combine all of the ingredients. Serve as a treat.

Yield: 1 treat; 50 calories.

Slim-line Cuisine

½ cup cooked chicken, chopped
1 tablespoon steamed carrots, chopped
¼ cup cooked oatmeal
1 teaspoon Miller's bran

In a bowl, combine the chicken, carrots, and oatmeal. Sprinkle with the bran. Mix and serve.

Yield: 2 meals; 165 calories per meal.

Liver-lover Delight

½ cup water
4 ounces calf's liver, chopped
1 tablespoon low-fat cottage cheese

In a saucepan heat the water to a boil. Add the liver and cook for 2 minutes. Remove liver to a bowl and let cool. Add the cottage cheese, mix, and serve warm, not hot.

Yield: 1 meal; 225 calories.

Nonfat Cat

1 handful high-quality, lower-calorie dry cat food
   (such as Iams Less Active)
1 egg yolk, cooked
1 tablespoon low-fat yogurt
1 teaspoon cod liver oil

In a bowl, combine all of the ingredients. Serve.

Yield: 2 meals; 200 calories per meal.

Mighty Mung

⅓ cup carrots, grated
⅓ cup beets, grated
⅓ cup fresh parsley, minced
¼ cup cooked millet
½ teaspoon garlic, minced
1 tablespoon mung bean sprouts, chopped

Place the vegetables in a bowl. Stir in the millet and garlic. Stir in the mung bean sprouts. Serve.

Yield: 2 meals; 200 calories per meal.

Good Exercise (Do Not Feed)

2 tablespoons dried catnip
One 5-inch-square piece of cloth
One 36-inch-long string

Place catnip in the middle of cloth. Bring all four sides of cloth together and tie with one end of the string to make a ball. Place the ball on the ground and pull it around the room. The cat will chase the ball and get some exercise. And so will you!

The expected life span of the average cat is 12 to 15 years. As a cat ages, his or her need for calories slowly decreases, protein requirements lessen, obesity becomes a potential health risk, and a less acute sense of smell leads to more discriminating eating behavior.

As your cat ages, your goal should be to maintain his or her ideal weight. This means you will probably have to reduce the quantity of food you offer at each meal by 10 to 20 percent over a period of years. You should pay close attention to your cat's silhouette and contours, and work with your veterinarian, if necessary, to create an ideal balanced diet. Since older cats have less need for protein, you may be advised to cut protein by 20 percent in your cat's later years, and you may be advised to add a vitamin-mineral supplement to replace nutrients lost by the reduction in the quantity of food you feed your cat.

By offering a variety of recipes in this chapter, you can be assured that your older cat is getting a nutritionally balanced diet. Remember that these dishes can easily be divided into two portions, and that the second portion can be kept overnight in the refrigerator for use the next day.

Grand Daddy of Sole

⅓ cup cooked sole fillet, boned and chopped
¼ cup cooked barley
1 teaspoon steamed carrots, chopped
½ teaspoon nonfat milk

In a bowl, combine the fish and barley. Stir in the carrots. Place the dried milk in a small bowl, stir in a little water, and pour over fish mixture. Serve.

Yield: 2 meals; 175 calories per meal.

Forever Young

¼ teaspoon safflower oil
1 teaspoon bell pepper, chopped
⅓ cup extra-lean ground chicken or turkey
½ teaspoon dried alfalfa

Heat the oil in a small skillet and sauté the bell pepper until tender. Stir in the ground meat and cook for 2 minutes. Stir in the alfalfa. Place the mixture in a bowl and let cool. Serve warm, not hot.

Yield: 1 meal; 165 calories.

Liver and Garlic with Cheese

½ cup water
1 whole chicken liver
1 clove garlic, crushed
1 tablespoon seeded tomato, chopped and peeled
2 teaspoons low-fat cottage cheese

In a small saucepan, boil the water. Add the liver and cook for 2 minutes. Remove the liver and let cool. Place the garlic in a bowl and stir in the tomato and cottage cheese. Chop the liver into bite-sized pieces and stir into the bowl. Serve.

Yield: 1 meal; 240 calories.

Good for What Ails Ya

1 cup water
1 chicken bouillon cube (low-sodium)
⅓ cup cooked chicken
¼ cup steamed carrots and green beans, chopped
¼ cup cooked brown rice or barley
¼ teaspoon fresh parsley, minced

In a small sauce pan, boil the water, add the bouillon cube, and stir to dissolve. Lower the heat and add the chicken, vegetables, and rice or barley. Cook for 2 minutes. Place in a bowl and let cool. Top with the parsley. Serve warm, not hot.

Yield: 2 meals; 265 calories per meal.

Kitty Curry (Mild)

1 tablespoon water
Dash of curry powder
¼ cup cooked lamb, chopped
¼ cup cooked couscous
1 teaspoon steamed cauliflower, chopped
1 teaspoon steamed peas

In a saucepan, combine the water and curry powder. Stir in the lamb and couscous and warm over low heat for 2 minutes. Add a little more water if needed. Transfer the mixture to a bowl and stir in the cauliflower and peas. Mix in and let cool. Serve warm, not hot.

Yield: 2 meals; 215 calories per meal.

Old Man of the Tree

½ teaspoon safflower oil
4 ounces beef heart, chopped
1 tablespoon bell pepper, chopped
1 hard-boiled egg
1 teaspoon brewer's yeast

Heat the oil in a small skillet and sauté the beef heart and bell pepper for 1 minute, stirring constantly. In a bowl, chop the egg into bite-sized pieces and add the brewer's yeast. Mix in. Combine the beef heart and bell pepper with the egg. Let cool before serving.

Yield: 2 meals; 160 calories per meal.

Senior Superior

1 cooked lamb kidney, chopped
1 tablespoon steamed green beans, chopped
1 tablespoon steamed carrots, chopped
⅓ cup cooked barley
½ teaspoon safflower oil

In a bowl, combine all of the ingredients. Serve.

Yield: 2 meals; 250 calories per meal.

Oldie but a Goody

4 ounces cooked lean beef, chopped
1 egg yolk, cooked
¼ cup cooked brown rice
2 tablespoons steamed carrots, chopped
½ teaspoon steamed bone meal

In a bowl, combine the beef, egg yolk, and carrot. Stir in the steamed bone meal. Serve.

Yield: 2 meals; 300 calories per meal.

Aristocats

¼ cup cooked beef, chopped
⅓ cup cooked brown rice
¼ cup cooked asparagus tips, chopped
½ teaspoon fresh ginger, grated
2 drops soy sauce (low-sodium)

In a bowl, combine the beef and rice. Add the asparagus tips and stir. Stir in the ginger and soy sauce. Serve.

Yield: 2 meals; 250 calories per meal.

67

INDEX